DIGITAL MARKETING JOURNEY

A Beginner's Guide to Digital Marketing

ADENEKAN MAYOWA, ADEBAYO

DIGITAL MARKETING JOURNEY

A Beginner's Guide to Digital Marketing

This book is dedicated to everyone who encouraged me on my journey to creating a career path in digital marketing. To clients, friends, and family members who supported my endeavour to build a digital marketing business that help businesses and individuals to be their best and to succeed. A big cheer also to everyone who is determined to make the most of their lives by leveraging the opportunities available online. May you find the journey easy.

ACKNOWLEDGMENTS

A Digital Marketing Journey was a team effort from start to finish. I'd like to thank my clients, friends, and family members who played key roles in helping me get this book from start to finish.

My partner, who fights along side me everyday.

My teammates at work—who constantly remind me of the importance of following my dream without giving up.

My profound gratitude to my parents; Mr and Mrs Adenekan, for the support and love.

Also, I want to appreciate my Father in heaven for the privilege given unto me to write and publish this book.

CONTENTS

"Every Knowledge, Principles and
Theories have a history, that bridges
your acquaintance into the workings of
the business world."
— **ADENEKAN MAYOWA ADEBAYO**

SUMMARY

*This chapter is designed by the Author to amass
you into the world of digital marketing, subtly
introducing you to real time facts in a step-by-step
learning process, enriching your grounds with a
fertile beginning for growth. In order to prepare
you for further chapters, the Author is modeling
his journey in the digital marketing space as a
compass to give the reader the directions of the
book and in the context addressing their
problems.*

5 TYPES OF **DIGITAL MARKETING**

SEARCH ENGINE OPTIMIZATION

CONTENT MARKETING

SOCIAL MEDIA MARKETING

MOBILE MARKETING

EMAIL MARKETING

CHAPTER ONE

INTRODUCTION

Growth is a very important element of life. As we record changes, it enables us to recognize the difference between where we were and where we are today, allowing us to correct many mistakes and adopt new thoughts that will help us forge into the future.

The journey of every businessman, entrepreneur, artist, craftsman, digital marketer, and creative writer started the same way. From a single thought that grew into an idea and consequently became a business empire.

My name is Adenekan M. Adebayo and my journey in the digital space took the same shape in 2011. I have a B.Sc. in mass communication, an M.Sc. in public relations and digital marketing. Other professional certifications include Google Ads Certification and Dubai KHDA Digital Media Certification. I have built myself up by acquiring more skills over the years since 2011. Over the years, I have grown to become a positive role model to many young digital marketers. In a bid to do my part in the contribution to knowledge, I decided to write a book that inspires the confidence of young digital marketers in a twelve-chapter book. I had to come up with a relatable content seeing the oceans of misleading digital marketing guides on the internet, that tend to window dress the facts with attractive statistics without telling you about real-life challenges and the tight competition that you are bound to face in the digital space on your way to the top.

In one of my publications in 2022 on the national dailies titled *"Advice to Young Aspiring Digital Marketers,"* I reiterated how my burning passion for the digital market fueled my success, aimed at showing young enthusiast my strong will, motivate them into success in their quest to grow in the same line of my career and that's what this book is all about. Changing the narrative by helping beginner avoid so many bourgeoise process and mistakes most digital marketers have made on their journey to the top of their career.

Before we delve into the book, I would like to define some of the important key terms relevant to this chapter.

1. What is Digital Marketing?

2. Types of Digital Marketing

What is Digital Marketing?

It is the marketing of products or services using digital channels to reach consumers. The key objective is to promote brands through various forms of digital media. In a layman's term, digital marketing is simply using the normal marketing techniques for the promotion of the use of services and your brand using electronic devices, social media, and other technologies and techniques that are available on the internet.

It is the process of attracting leads by providing content that is helpful to them that will organically lead to engagement. What this means is that we are talking about inbound marketing. They are focusing on generating content that your target audience, the people you want to reach, would like, find interesting, relevant, educational, or enlightening. When they consume your content; videos, images, or audio; they get drawn to your brand because you've given them some level of information that they already like. Think about inbound marketing as paid media. Inbound marketing is a pull strategy because you are controlling your content and drawing people into your brand, getting them to: most times when you hear.

According to Kotler and Amstrong, digital marketing is a form of direct marketing that links consumers with sellers electronically using interactive technologies like emails, websites, online forums and newsgroups, interactive television, mobile communications, etc. I see digital marketing as a means of achieving personal or business goals. The sole reason for starting a project, planning and designing a roadmap, and creating strategies is to achieve the goal of the project. Take, for example, an organization with different departments such as Finance, Admin, IT, Consultancy, etc. All the departments were set up by the organization in order to take advantage of their synergy to achieve their business goals.

What Is The Significance Of Digital Marketing?

Digital marketing allows you to reach a larger audience than traditional methods and target prospects who are most likely to purchase your product or service. Furthermore, it is often less expensive than traditional advertising and allows you to measure success on a daily basis and pivot as needed.

There are several significant advantages to using digital marketing:

- You can target only the prospects who are most likely to buy your product or service.
- It is less expensive than outbound marketing methods.
- Digital marketing levels the playing field in your industry, allowing you to compete with larger brands.
- Digital marketing can be measured.
- A digital marketing strategy is easier to adapt and change.
- Digital marketing can be enhanced.
- Digital marketing can boost your conversion rate and lead quality.
- With digital marketing, you can engage audiences at every stage.

1. You can concentrate your efforts on prospects who are most likely to buy your product or service.

You have little control over who sees your advertisement if you place it on TV, in a magazine, or on a billboard. Of course, certain demographics can be measured, such as the magazine's typical readership or the demographics of a specific neighborhood, but it's still largely a guessing game.

In contrast, digital marketing allows you to identify and target a highly specific audience as well as send that audience personalized, high-converting marketing messages.

For example, you could use social media targeting features to show social media ads to a specific audience based on variables like age, gender, location, interests, networks, or behaviors. You could also use PPC or SEO strategies to serve ads to users who have expressed interest in your product or service, or who have searched for specific keywords related to your industry.

Finally, digital marketing allows you to conduct the research required to identify your buyer persona, as well as refine your marketing strategy over time to ensure you're reaching prospects who are most likely to buy. Best of all, digital marketing enables you to market to subsets of your larger target audience. This is especially useful if you sell multiple products or services to different buyer personas.

2. It is less expensive than traditional outbound marketing methods.

Digital marketing allows you to track campaigns on a daily basis and reduce the amount of money you spend on a specific channel if it isn't delivering a high ROI. The same cannot be said for traditional forms of advertising. It makes no difference how well your billboard performs—whether it converts or not.

Furthermore, with digital marketing, you have complete control over where you spend your money. Rather than paying for PPC campaigns, you could invest in design software to create high-converting Instagram content. A digital marketing strategy allows you to pivot on the fly, ensuring you never waste money on channels that don't perform well.

For example, if you work for a small business with a low budget, you could try investing in social media, blogging, or SEO—three tactics that can provide a high ROI even with a tiny investment.

3. Digital marketing levels the playing field in your sector, allowing you to compete with larger brands.

If you work for a small firm, you will almost certainly find it difficult to compete with the major companies in your field, many of whom have millions of dollars to invest in television advertisements or nationwide campaigns. Fortunately, clever digital marketing campaigns provide numerous opportunities to outrank major businesses.

For example, you may find long-tail keywords related to your product or service and develop high-quality content to help you rank in search engines for those keywords. Search engines don't care which brand is the most popular; instead, they emphasize information that resonates most with the target demographic.

4. Digital marketing may be tracked.

Digital marketing can provide you with a full, end-to-end picture of all the metrics that are important to your business, such as impressions, shares, views, clicks, and time on page. This is one of the most significant advantages of digital marketing. While traditional advertising can be effective for some purposes, its main shortcoming is its lack of measurability.

Digital marketing, unlike most offline marketing

initiatives, allows marketers to observe exact outcomes in real time.

If you've ever placed an ad in a newspaper, you know how tough it is to determine how many people really switched to that page and read your ad. There's no way to determine for sure if that ad was responsible for any sales at all.

Digital marketing, on the other hand, allows you to track the ROI of virtually every facet of your marketing activities.

Here are a couple of such examples:

Website Visits

Using digital analytics tools, accessible through marketing platforms such as HubSpot, you can monitor the precise number of individuals who have seen your website's homepage in real time.

Among other digital analytics data, you can see how many pages they viewed, what device they were using, and where they came from.

This knowledge allows you to prioritize which marketing channels to spend more or less time on based on the quantity of people that visit your website through those channels. For example, if organic search accounts for only 10% of your traffic, you know you'll need to invest some time in SEO to boost that percentage.

It's tough to identify how consumers are connecting with your brand before they meet with a salesperson or make a purchase using offline marketing. You may uncover trends and patterns in people's behavior with digital marketing before they reach the last stage of their buyer's journey, allowing you to make better educated decisions about how to attract them to your site right at the top of the sales funnel.

For example, there are more than fifteen types of digital marketing, but for the sake of this book, we will be discussing the following:

- Search Engine Optimization (SEO)
- Marketing on Social Media
- Content Marketing
- Email Marketing

 **SEO, OR SEARCH ENGINE OPTIMIZATION,**

The Google search engine provides a wealth of

information to anyone who is trying to find out about a product, individual, or organization. Once a search is launched, Google delivers results for your searches on the first page according to the keywords you used to search. This gives you an insight into the popular things people search for about your business or products. Making your website SEO friendly ensures that it is not excluded from the Google search engine. When your website appears on the Google search engine when customers search for your product, it means your website is SEO friendly.

Understanding SEO

Every digital marketer needs to understand how SEO works in order to improve a site's appearance on the Google search engine. The Google algorithm changes on a regular basis, and the digital marketer must keep this in mind. Think of Search Engine Optimization as a large store that has over one million products displayed on the shelves with just one store attendant who has the list of all the registered products and their descriptions. The challenge here is that some customers might not make enquiries according to the name of the products but by their functions, which puts those products with a good description at an advantage over others. That large store is Google, and the store keeper is the Google search engine. One of those ways of doing that includes:

- ***Content indexing:***

Looking at the same instance in the aforementioned point, Content Indexing is simply put, adding a name, description, and price tag, so it can be easily identified by the attendant to be able to serve the customer. In this case, those extra features are the index and the attendant Google search engine. The customer is the user of the Google search engine. Content indexing involves adding special features to your media files when publishing a post on your website in order to allow search engines to read it clearly. Including image alt text and text transcripts for audio and video content.

- ***Good link structure***

What happens here is that the attendant usually takes a stroll to each product stand to familiarize himself with the products in order to have a great record of all the products and services. Presumably, the route he takes to reach each product stand is the link. If the route is long, it might discourage him from visiting.

So, as illustrated above, if your site does not have a good link structure that allows search engines to successfully crawl your website, your contents will be pushed down on the list of Google search results. The solution is to format the links, sitemaps, and URLs to make them easily accessible by search engines.

- ***Keywords and keyword research***

Keywords are the words that help the Google search engine identify your niche. These keywords are added to your site's content and header. For example, a site that offers graphic design might want to use keywords like "graphic design" or "Adobe Photoshop" in their content, but due to a change in the algorithm of Google, adding too many keywords in your website's content will cause Google to de-rank your website or even skip the content. Writing rich content with a few keywords on the page and in the headers is now the best practice to rank your pages in search engines.

 ## MARKETING AND CONTENT CREATION

Content creation is the most important strategy in the digital marketing world. All other digital marketing depends on content marketing. Whether you are planning to launch an ad campaign on social media such as Facebook, Instagram, Twitter, or YouTube, you'll need to create or generate ideas targeting your buyers and build both visual and written content such as video script ideas, product descriptions, flyers, banners, and captions around your ideas in order to get the attention of your customers.

 ## MARKETING ON SOCIAL MEDIA:

As a digital marketer, your ultimate goal is to reach your potential customers through digital means. Social media presents that opportunity to marketers because of the increase in the number of people on social media. The most popular social media platforms among digital marketers include Twitter, Instagram, and Facebook, but Google My Business, eBay, and many others offer great features that support the promotion of our services and products. This opens you up to many other options, as a blend of two social media might be the brand break-through for your social media campaign.

In order to achieve that, a plan is required, a strategic approach to take advantage of the millions of users across the globe. One of the greatest challenges of marketing on social media is a lack of consistency. It's not just making a post and replying to comments; the content has to be consistent in order to keep new and old followers busy. Though there are tools available to help schedule posts, followers might sense there is no real person behind them and might not take the page seriously. Consistency does not just stop with creating posts; the brand has to be consistent with a particular style and maintain it across all their social media platforms. Social media marketers who create ads should be able to collect data from their dash board, analyze it, and measure the performance of their campaign. Such an analysis will provide an insight into whether the post is doing well or not, and an appropriate action should follow, to either discontinue the ad or just let it run. Analyzing your results helps you keep track of the entire project's trajectory; you can be able to calculate the return on investment. For instance, you were hired by a company to help promote their brand. The company has a plan to reach a total of 200k people in a month and a budget of 70k per ad. By keeping track of the ads' progress, you will be able to measure when the post has reached a total number of 200k. The company's return on investment is the 200k people reached using less than 70k.

"In the changing world of business, the everyday stiff competition and fight to win customers, Digital Marketing terminologies is our only tool of persuasion that evens the playing field for both large and small firms."
— **ADENEKAN MAYOWA ADEBAYO**

SUMMARY

The art of war is implied here, to arm the digital marketer with the necessary terminologies which will be used frequently in further chapters, sharpen their power of persuasion. Undoubtedly, this will help the reader to fully understand the topics, with the sole aim of helping the reader to communicate across various digital marketing disciplines more efficiently, increase their clarity of ambiguous digital marketing concepts.

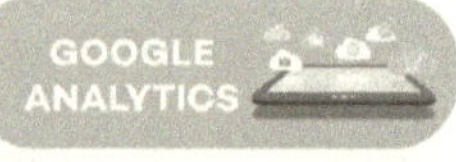

DIGITAL MARKETING TECHNOLOGIES

CHAPTER TWO
BASIC TERMINOLOGIES OF DIGITAL MARKETING

I have to admit that, even though I do not fancy the use of big words that will cause you to consult your dictionary every time, it is important to learn some of the basic terminology in this field. As a prospective digital marketer who intends to build a career around digital marketing, you have to learn and understand its uses if you want to be taken as a professional.

In the words of Vakulenko (1994), a term is a word or collocation that refers to a concept of science, technology, culture, sports, art, etc. Terminology is simply a group of words or semantics with specialized meaning or definitions that are set aside specially for a particular field or profession. These words were created out of the necessity to enable understanding and easy communication of a particular profession. Every profession has its own set of terminologies and those who practice such a profession often use them in their day-to-day activities.

In July 2018, I learned a very big lesson in digital marketing. I lost a massive product campaign job to a competitor, not because I wasn't good, but because I wasn't able to communicate my services to the clients in clear digital marketing terms. Some clients will dig into your websites and ask questions about your agency from your old clients. They need to be able to trust you with their money.

However, some clients are very thorough and might request a Zoom meeting, schedule a one-on-one conversation with their marketing department, or just choose to communicate with you by mail. The reason for doing that is for them to be able to access your understanding of the task, your ability to handle the task, and your plan.

However, they perceived me as an amateur due to my inability to communicate my plan, even though I had had experience handling similar jobs in the last two years.

The business of digital marketing is the business of communication; you communicate with your clients and sell your services to them in the best language that will describe the core importance of your values. When you have gotten the job to market your client's products, you still need to use the product to communicate with your target market through emails, product descriptions, and also verbal or on the phone persuasion. In order to achieve all these, you need to arm yourself with the right language that will bring out the thoughts, beauty, and value behind the product or services.

If you are self-educating like I did while starting up, then you surely need to learn some good terminology. Because you will feel like a sailor lost at sea or an explorer who has lost their way while reading up on digital marketing materials due to the strange language.

This will allow you to search for materials relevant to your research and help you easily adopt when attending a tutorial or a master class.

Therefore, I have put together a good number of important terms that will help you understand the digital marketing process that I'm going to introduce you to in the next chapter and set you on your way to success. These terms have been classified according to the types of digital marketing as earlier discussed.

Why is it important to learn digital marketing terms?

- To boost your confidence in the digital world,
- To improve communication and increase understanding between the digital marketer and the client,
- To enable digital marketers to translate data and make use of available resources.
- To deal with people of different business backgrounds and to function perfectly in any team or group.
- It helps the digital marketer to have a well-defined brand voice and creates a spot-on corporate identity in such a way that any customer can relate to it and identify it among thousands of other competing brands.
- It helps to create great customer satisfaction and a lasting impression as the communication is very clear and it reduces further queries from a customer

and the need for customer support.

- It reduces costs and saves the digital marketer time in striking a deal when negotiating and sealing an ad campaign deal, as there will be fewer corrections and reviews. The project will have a smooth transition from start to finish.

Content Marketing Terminologies

- *Conversion rate optimization (CRO)*

CRO involves defining your site's goal, collecting and analyzing visitors' data, and doing everything else to increase your site's conversation rate.

- *Email marketing*

Email marketing is the process of reaching out to your target audience through well-structured messages tailored specifically to their interests.

- *Geofencing*

Geofencing is a term that refers to the process of marketing your product to a particular set of people in a defined geographical location. The marketer maps out the area where he wants to target, and the ads will only be seen by the people in that defined location.

- *Lead nurturing*

Here, relationships are the means of marketing your product. There is a large portion of your customer base who buy because they have developed trust in your product. Marketers nurture such relationships that in the near future will become clients.

- *Local SEO*

"Local SEO" is when you optimize your website to rank in local results. It includes Claiming your Google My Business listing, writing pages based on local keywords, and more.

- *Page speed optimization*

Page speed refers to the time it takes for your site to load a page. Users get discouraged if a site lags too much and takes too much time to process their requests, especially on e-commerce sites during check-outs. A good way to reduce too much lag and increase your site's loading speed is to compress media files and regularly clean up your HTML code.

- *SEO*

SEO is the practice of optimizing your website for search engines and users. The end goal of SEO is to help your content rank highly in search engines like Google. So that your target audience finds you when they search for a term that you target with your content. SEO helps you rank organically, or without paying for rankings.

- *Advertising on social media*

Social media advertising allows you to create and distribute ads for your products. Or services on a range of social platforms, including Facebook, Twitter, Instagram, LinkedIn, and more. Most platforms have an ad platform baked right in.

- *Marketing on social media*

Social Media Marketing is the process of using social media platforms to reach a target set of people known as an audience or followers through your content. That could be either text, pictures, or videos, particularly relevant to your business. Let's say, for example, you have a website for streaming movies. Your content should be about new movie updates, trends, and reviews. This practice helps you to grow your brand and create awareness that will drive traffic to your blog. The most popular social media platforms are Twitter, Facebook, YouTube, Instagram, and YouTube.

- *Voice search optimization*

Voice search optimization is when you adjust your content to target users that search using a voice search device. You speak differently out loud than you would while typing a query, voice search optimization helps you optimize for verbal queries

- *Website design*

Website design is the practice of creating a user-friendly website that informs users about your business, products, and services.

"The three stages of growth I have come
to realize is idea, conception, growth
and continuity and that is the direction
every business should take."
— Adenekan Mayowa Adebayo

SUMMARY

In this chapter the author addresses the need to understand the process involved in digital marketing, highlighting the customer journey in clear simple context. Also, using the concept of process to explain the need for every digital marketer to undergo stages of development. Reiterating the need for a step-by-step approach to a problem that converges into a solution. The author specifies that understanding the digital marketing process puts you in the world of customers or clients, their actions and behaviour.

DIGITAL MARKETING PROCESS

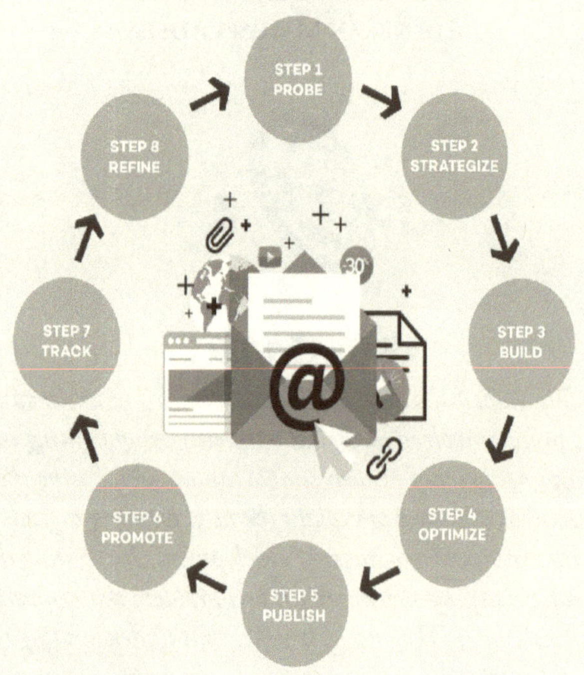

CHAPTER THREE

DIGITAL MARKETING PROCESSES

Process
DEFINITION

A process can be a gradual change, a series of actions marked with actions or recorded operations, interconnected in ascending order that eventually converges to achieve a result. a mouse in a puzzle cage with five compartments. In order to open the door to the second compartment of the cage, the rat has to eat a cheese to enter the second room, then remove another obstacle. Note that all the action of the mice is geared towards going to the fifth compartment for the big reward. The digital marketing process is the same way, and in this case, you, as the freelancer, agency, or entrepreneur, are the observer that monitors and supervises the entire process.

What is the Digital Marketing Process?

I call the digital marketing process the ABC of digital marketing. The process means to a digital marketer what the alphabet means to a learner of English. It simply breaks down the how, where, and when of digital marketing. No matter the definition of digital marketing that you may know, two things stand out: project starts and project ends. Whatever activities or strategies you use in between the beginning of a project and the end, are termed the "digital marketing process." A conventional digital marketing strategy might involve research, creating, promoting, analyzing, optimizing, but it is not the same in all cases.

The Digital Marketing Process Is Useful In The Following Ways:

1. To create a digital marketing campaign for a product, business, brand, or individual, one needs a strategy called the Digital Marketing Process.
2. It helps to map out the entire process of the campaign from start to finish.
3. The digital marketing process helps you to take control of your campaign every step of the way.

Who Can Use The Digital Marketing Process?

The users of the digital marketing process include the following set of people:

1. If you are a digital marketing agency and you offer digital marketing services to others, known as clients,

2. A freelancer who has been trained in digital marketing but does not own a firm and intends to market his client's business on digital media.

3. An entrepreneur who intends to market his own products online.

4. A person who is employed by an agency and it is his duty to create digital marketing campaigns for the client that has hired his agency.

The digital marketing process makes it possible for the DM to track the progress of the campaign's every phase.

The Digital Marketing Process

Stage One: Research and Information Gathering

Stage Two: Creation of Content for the Campaign

Stage Three: Publicize

Stage Four: Analysis

Step 5: Optimize

STAGE ONE: RESEARCH AND GATHERING OF DATA

Of course, carrying out research on a particular product is the first important stage of every project. Research will assist you in launching the appropriate inquiry about the product you intend to market to the general public. For example, Mayor Pharmaceutical Company hired your service as a DM to help promote their flag brand Amino Gentaz, a product that cures diabetes. The very first thing to do is to launch an enquiry into the product and the firm, and gather information regarding the products that will help you to easily create powerful content to use for the campaign. Such information may include:

1. About the Product:

This should satisfy all enquiries about the products in terms of name and nature of the product, size, colour, and contents of the product. This information you can simply get from the client or research about them using the internet.

2.About the business:

This enquiry covers everything you need to know about the business, from their structure to their digital marketing goals, their target customers, and their budget.

3.About Your Target Customers:

Researching your target customers helps you understand their age, demography, region and, if possible, spending power. That will give you a direction on how to direct your campaign, whether to show it to people of all ages or target a particular age bracket or people in a particular region. Though, in the case of digital products with universal usage, such as e-books, region targeting may not be an issue unless the product was written specifically for a specific group of people.

4.About Online Competition

Research into your client's online competition will help you gather information that will put your campaign ahead of your client's competition even though they are both selling similar products. If a product does not meet the criteria of their digital marketing strategies, some digital marketers provide brand consultancy. Most digital marketers advise the client to hire a brand consultant or rebrand their product due to high competition. The information gathered from the research stage is the data the DM will use in the second stage (pre-launch stage) to create content for the campaign.

STAGE TWO: CONTENT CREATION OR CREATION

This is the next stage in the research process. The contents that have been gathered from the client's business, client's products, target customers, and competition will be used to create content in readiness for the launching of the marketing campaign.

The contents include: strategies to be used for the campaign, marketing plan, objectives of digital marketing, digital identities;

- *The Objectives of Digital Marketing:*

The objectives of digital marketing include knowing what the client intends to promote. Is it a product or service or simply to increase their online presence? This all depends on the client. In the event that a client does not know how to go about it, the digital marketer might as well consult for the client. The digital marketer must try by all means to unify both the objectives of the client and the objectives of the campaign in order to achieve perfect harmony and avoid cases of misplaced priorities. Therefore, different goals and objectives should be set for different projects as organizational objectives differ from firm to firm.

- *Marketing Strategies for the Campaign:*

These strategies include branding strategies, content strategies, positioning strategies, and digital marketing channel strategies. These strategies are necessary at the pre-launch stage of your campaign after setting your goals and objectives.

Content strategy is important when the client's identities have been created and there's a need to niche down. This will help the DM to know what content to post, how to post and when to post it, while the digital marketing channels allow the digital marketer the flexibility to explore other means of promoting the client's products or services, such as email marketing, social media and YouTube. The strategy to be adopted depends on the information gotten from the objectives of digital marketing. For instance, if the objective clearly states that the client plans to reach 200k people within a period of 1 week, the DM will select the best digital marketing strategies to reach the target goal of the client.

- *A Digital Marketing Plan*

The digital marketing plan breaks down the projects into details with a defined time stamp attached to each activity. This way, it's easier for the DM to know how long it took to execute each stage.

- *Creating Primary Digital Identities:*

The whole network of marketing is aimed at selling an organization's reputation, a product, or services. This is why every lead from a campaign leads to what we refer to as a digital platform known as a landing page. This is usually an online store, a company's website, blog, or App where the target audience is supposed to take action by buying a product or subscribing to a service. For instance, you have mounted four signboards directing people from a stadium every two miles for ten miles, and it leads two people to your store that sells sports equipment and consumables. The store gives your business serious credibility and fosters a sense of trust and continuity.

For businesses that want to sell their products through major e-commerce portals, creating digital identities can be optional. But, it's better to at least have a website to establish some credibility for your business.

STAGE THREE: PUBLICIZE

After your primary digital identities are fully ready, you will start promoting them. That means you want relevant people to start coming to your primary digital identities. This is also called generating relevant traffic. Relevant traffic is an important word here.

The more relevant traffic you get to your website, the more conversions you can expect. Your options to promote your website/blog/app will be:

1. Search Engines
2. Display Network
3. Ecommerce Portals

4. Social Media
5. Email
6. Messaging
7. Affiliate

The above are also known as "digital marketing channels," through which you need to promote your primary digital identities (website/blog/app). There are sub-channels and networks within some of the channels mentioned above.

Which channels, subchannels, and networks to use, as well as whether to use organic or inorganic promotions, will be determined during the Digital Marketing Strategy creation stage.

STAGE 4: EXAMINE

Once you create your primary digital identities and start promoting them through various digital marketing channels, it's time to start monitoring your performance. Analyzing is like looking at the outcome of your digital marketing work. You will receive analytics for your primary digital identities as well as the channels through which you have done the promotions.

The most important and ultimate analytics for any business is the analytics of your website, blog, or app. Google Analytics is widely popular for generating analytics of your primary digital identities. The 4 major sections of Google Analytics are:

- Audiences
- Acquisition
- Behavior
- Conversion

"A person with many skills, is one that is journeying down the roads to perfection."
— Adenekan Mayowa Adebayo

SUMMARY

Skills are the new trend in our digitized economy, here the Author has filtered down the digital marketing skills that you need, specifically tailored to your needs using the digital marketing process stages. This will allow a digital marketing enthusiast to be able to concentrate on the important skills that are needed for in order to launch successful marketing campaign for a client.

Digital Marketing Hard Skills

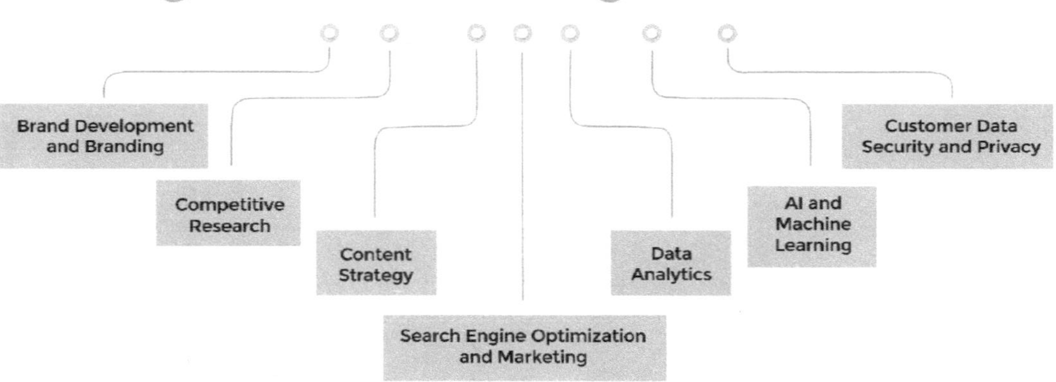

CHAPTER FOUR

SKILLS YOU NEED TO SURVIVE AS A DIGITAL MARKETER

Though your survival in the business of marketing is dependent on so many other things, having the necessary skills is key to your success. In January 2012, I was self-educating myself on digital marketing skills, reading articles, watching YouTube videos and reading all the e-books I could find. I learned a lot of skills without much guidance, which was a good thing, but at some stage in your digital marketing career, learning the relevant skills that will allow you to launch a successful marketing campaign is important. I had the skills but just didn't even know what to do with them.

Why is it important to learn digital marketing skills? Those skills help to improve your level of efficiency and professionalism. For those who own a digital marketing firm and have employees, it helps you easily supervise their input, monitor results, and analyze the outcome of every campaign, whether you are a freelancer or work for a digital marketing firm.

By learning how to be an effective digital marketer, you can ensure you're delivering the message you intend to — both personally and professionally — and seeing the desired results. Developing these skills will also help you better monitor the work your employees are putting out, so you can understand whether the campaigns your company implements are optimized for success, as well as identify areas of improvement.

It can get overwhelming sometimes, keeping up with the numerous skills or knowing what stage to apply them. So, I began to study the processes of digital marketing, and discovered that although it's important to learn as many skills as possible, it's best to specialize in only a few. Well, how do you know what few skills to specialize in? Because most e-books and online articles will only list numerous skills and will never tell you when or how to apply them. The step-by-step process of digital marketing provides you with the framework that allows you to know what skills you need, allowing you to shred some of the skills that are not tailored to your strategies.

STEPS	DIGITAL MARKETING PROCESS	SKILLS NEEDED
1.	Research	Competitive Research
2.	Create	Content Writing, Basic Design Skills and Branding
3.	Promote	SEO, ADS., Email Marketing Skills
4.	Analyze	Data Analysis
5.	Optimize	Customer Relationship Skills

1. Brand Development And Branding:

After the outbreak of the COVID-19 Pandemic, a lot of new businesses sprung up, including online stores and services-oriented businesses. This affected a lot of companies who do not have an online presence as most businesses use digital platforms as a way of communicating with their customers. Most of these businesses were able to penetrate the market with a great business identity or personality, which is unusual since most large organizations never paid attention to digital marketing.

This prompted the need for digital marketers to add branding and brand development to their list of skills.

Accordingly, the marketing giant HubSpot posited that "a brand identity is made up of what your brand says, what your values are, how you communicate your product, and what you want people to feel when they interact with it." Essentially, your brand identity is the personality of your business and a promise to your customers. "

In my opinion, brand identity is the consistent poetry of business, the sublime description, and the beautiful message from a business to its customers. This is because the brand identity helps the business to tell the story of their corporate responsibility, the nature of their product, how they have added value to those products, and the lifechanging experience they will get from using your product. Having brand identity skills will help you understand the need for a consistent combination of company colour, website design, and logo design.

Brand development, on the other hand, is the overall growth of a brand. Digital marketers usually develop a brand from a logo, which is foundational to the practice of branding. By following the brand style guide usually provided by the client, but in the case where there's no existing brand style guide, the digital marketer would have to handle the responsibility of bringing in a brand identity expert or designing it himself since some digital marketers have graphic design skills.

Also, brand identity will help the DM understand the brand voice. For instance, the brand voice is the tone and structure of the client's content. For instance, the tone of the article of Forbes might be persuading and bold, with a particular text size and arrangement, and it's consistent across all of their publications.

Importance:

- According to research done by Fundera, it was concluded that about 63% of business transactions come from existing customers, and 43 percent of customers spend more on brands that they feel loyal to, which is an indication that once customers understand what a product is or who the company behind that product is, they can grow to become loyal ambassadors of the business and build their trust around your identity.

- Also, it helps Conversely, brand development also helps companies understand who their customers are. In doing so, it empowers them to connect with shoppers and make a clear, memorable impression on their target base.
- It helps a digital marketer to better craft advertising strategies that represent their client's brand, allowing them to deliver a great campaign capable of boosting sales and customer preference.

2. Competitive Research

Research is key to launching a new project. Digital marketers need this skill to be able to recognize and collect useful data about a brand's major competitors. By analyzing the competition, you will be able to understand their marketing strategies, sales and products and how to be a step ahead of them. This will give the brand a competitive advantage over other brands. Thus, this involves the digital marketer following up on news about the competitors and their rivals, and even subscribing to their newsletter to understand all their schedules.

Importance:

- Competitive marketing research gives a digital marketer an insight into the online behaviour of the competitor's brand.
- It helps the digital marketer easily spot the brand's weaknesses and adjust to them immediately.
- The digital marketer will tailor his digital strategies based on the analysis from competitive research.

3.Content Strategy:

In the course of every campaign, there should be a strategic approach to content marketing. This is one of the most critical skills for a digital marketer to have. The content strategy helps you to achieve two things at the same time: enlighten the customer about the product through tailored content that will lead them to understand your versatility in that niche and Though content might be perceived as self-promotional, it plays a major role in converting the action of a visiting customer.

For instance, let's take, for instance, a company that produces a special seasoning and sponsors a cooking show that uses their products. Once the show goes viral, the promotion of the seasoning also goes viral too. The show was initiated with the sole intent of selling out the special season. Due to the content strategy, the business will witness a huge increase in sales over a long period of time.

This simply implies that content strategy is not about flooding customers with the direct promotion of your product, but finding a way to show them how the seasoning works through the show. This content should also be able to educate and satisfy unanswered questions about the product. A perfect platform for such content includes YouTube, Instagram, and Facebook.

Statistics from HubSpot's 2020 State of Marketing Report support this claim. According to them, content marketing takes 70 percent of marketers' investments. While roughly 60% of those polled agreed that content marketing is an important component of their strategy.

4. Data Analytics

Data analytics is a powerful skill that any digital marketer needs. Data analytics involves the ability to translate data into competitive advantage. This data gives the digital marketer an insight into how the customers interact with the products; why there is an abandonment of carts; and the overall engagement of the products. This data is collected from the various campaign channels such as websites, social media, and YouTube. Professionally, in the digital world, most data about the market size of a particular industry, the revenue, the number of users of particular products, and the behaviour of the customers in terms of their interests and preferences are gotten from the analysis of data by professional data analysts, which tells you how important it is to develop the skill.

Conclusively, the rising number of investments in analytics shows that it is paramount to most businesses. Digitalization has shown so many businesses that they can be able to measure their brand's performance and see how many people are interested in them by analyzing data from their campaign.

According to the market size of marketing analysis presented by Mordor Intelligence, analytics has a revenue size of $2.3 billion in the year 2019. It is expected to grow at a compound annual growth rate (CAGR) of 14 percent between now and 2025, reaching $4.23 billion. This shows the rising need for market analysis is taking a positive trend in its demand and is not slowing down anytime soon.

5.Marketing and Search Engine Optimization

Search engines such as Google often suggest words to users according to key words used. Google often crawls websites that have those keywords in their content to the first page of their search results. Appearing on Google's first page gives you an edge over others based on your content. Having the skills of Search Engine Optimization and Marketing (SEO) helps you to create content that is search engine friendly.

Now, in the case where you are hired to promote a company's products and you have created great content for the website, without a good search engine optimization strategy, that product will not be visible to the customers and may never meet their sales target.

Though, recently, the search engine algorithm is after very rich and unique content, and littering your content with keywords can cause the search engine to ignore your content. Nevertheless, a website's content should still receive organic content from Google. SEO knowledge opens you up to the use of the Google search console to submit your sitemap, which will allow Google to crawl your site and drive traffic to your site when the demand arises. For digital marketers, understanding SEO is critical to success in today's search-engine-driven buying environment.

Personal Qualities Required of a Digital Marketer

Empathy:

Being empathetic puts the digital marketer in the shoes of the customer. This skill is important as it helps you get under the skin of your customers to understand what drives them to purchase your product and what their concerns and feelings are.

Curiosity

This skill has led many digital marketers to discover many strategies that may change the course of their career. Curiosity opens the DM to new ideas regarding products and customers.

Curiosity helps to sharpen the marketing instincts of

the digital marketer when it comes to making decisions about the brand.

Persuasiveness

The importance of persuasion makes intuitive sense—after all, marketing is all about persuasive communication. If you understand how to convince people to trust your brand and its products, you have one of the characteristics of a great marketer.

But let's clarify a key point — the power of persuasion isn't just about making a sale; it is about influencing how a customer feels. After the sale, too. When a customer concludes a transaction, they should walk away feeling satisfied and excited about their purchase.

"In the business world, business relationships nurtured and maintained are valuable asset a company or an individual can own, because it on that foundation that the pre-sale of future business are negotiated."
— ADENEKAN MAYOWA ADEBAYO

SUMMARY

Exposing the interactions that happens within the world of Digital marketing helps the reader to understanding the web of activities and how to tap into it. Imminently turning around your views, recognizing the important moves to make that will turn you into a digital marketing rock star, coaxing a road map for yourself that will guide you to success.

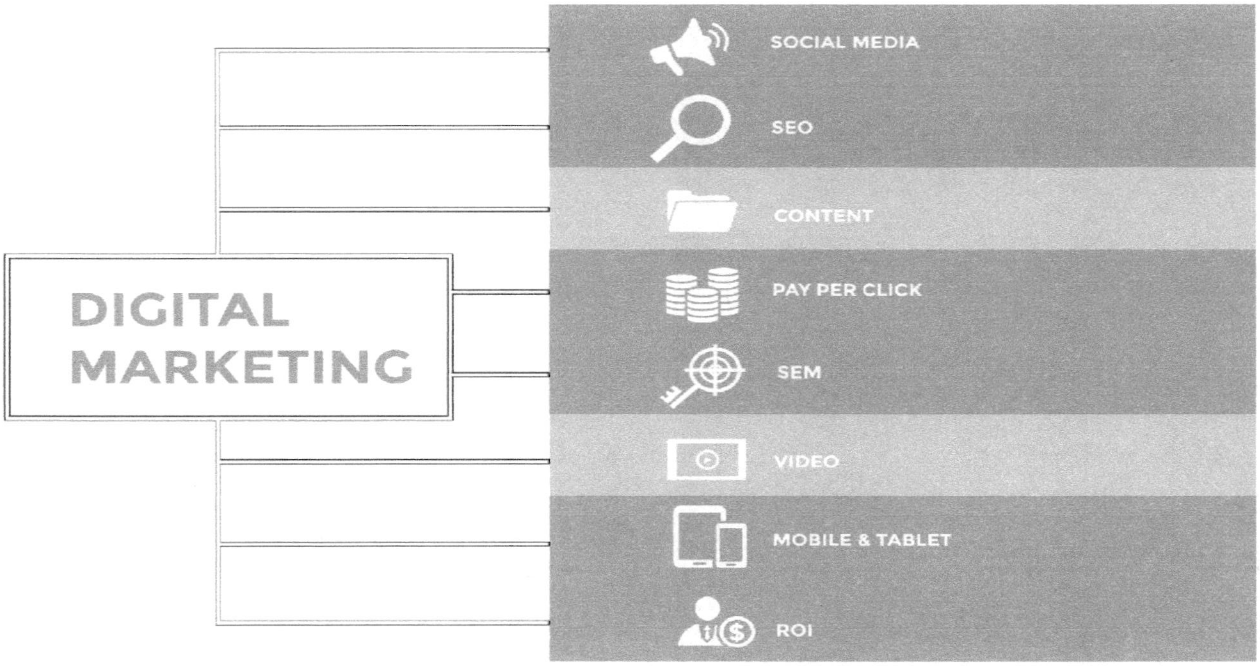

DIGITAL MARKETING
SOCIAL MEDIA
SEO
CONTENT
PAY PER CLICK
SEM
VIDEO
MOBILE & TABLET
ROI

CHAPTER FIVE

UNDERSTANDING THE DIGITAL MARKETING WORLD

In my second year at university, I had already figured out what I wanted to do when I got out of school. I knew what I could do and what I could not. Therefore, I understood the areas that I was lacking and needed to work on them. One of my most outstanding abilities is my love for the digital space and how so many beautiful images and videos caught my attention while souring the internet. I could not deny how engaging and compelling those advertisements were. You will find yourself clicking the link even when you don't need the products. I thought that was powerful and wanted to understand the magic behind it to be able to get people to take action and perhaps get them to buy.

I have been seeing random ads online and always wondered how they were created, the brand behind them, and who those products were actually made for. Was it for just me? Why does it change from time to time? Those inquisitions kept growing on me. But no one ever explained them to me in a way that allowed me to grow into the concept and bring myself to understand the process. While in school, I used to sell used phones to support myself financially and understand how it was difficult to persuade a customer to buy a single product, especially when it's not new.

Sometimes you face serious underpricing from customers depending on the shape in which the last user left it. So, I discovered most of them often complain about the looks of the phone even more than they do about its functionalities. I guess I owe that to the globalized world and the fashion craze.

I began to repackage the phones, changing the casing and making them look new. That action alone immensely increased the value of the phone, and I was able to upsell the same phone and also cover the cost of the packaging. I was able to break through the market and break even because of the customer analytics I gathered and how I used their feedback to create a product that met the needs of my target market, which were the users of second-new phones.

In the words of Adrian Hillary, a great digital marketer, "A good image is a very competitive tool of visual bargain that puts a product in the light of an easy, unarguable buy". Adrian's position was the same thought I had when I stumbled on Digital Marketing. A tool that could help me get a product in front of thousands of people who need it.

I started carrying out research online, in newspapers, magazines, and e-books to read more about my newly found obsession; I attended seminars; volunteered; and attended online classes and training.

Stepping into the digital marketing world, one should have it in the back of his mind that it's a growing market and attracts lots of competitors. The world of digital marketing is a world where only two sets of people exist: the advertising company and the

From my perspective, it is a space with a giant pool of beautifully branded products competing for the attention of their various rational target markets. As a digital marketer, in order to gain a full insight into the digital marketing world and understand its operations, one must first understand the following elements and how they are interconnected and how they interact with each other:

I discovered that the entire digital marketing revolves around these elements, and I have studied carefully their interactions and the interdependencies between them. I have broken them down into:

- The Digital Marketer (The Advertising Agency)
- The Client
- The Target Market
- The Product
- The Competitor
- The Customers

1. The Digital Marketer:

As an industry newcomer in the Digital Marketing world, I was bombarded with so many terminologies that I missed the simple yet important things. I had no idea how a digital marketer truly functions and fits into the numerous roles (creative thinking, planning, and strategy) that are involved in digital marketing. So, it was difficult for me to place myself and narrow down my capabilities, identify my strengths and weaknesses, because of the numerous things one has to learn to become a digital marketer. I discovered that you do not learn every conceivable digital marketing skill because you want to handle everything yourself, but to have an overall knowledge in order to allow you to make rational decisions with a wider scope of things.

Therefore, simply put, anyone who uses digital channels to reach customers, build brand awareness, and promote products and services is a digital marketer, and I therefore consider myself one. The digital marketer or the digital marketing agency has the most interactions with clients due to their importance. These clients include manufacturing companies, retailers, corporate organizations, individuals, and government agencies who either sell products or offer services. Every digital marketer's dream is to land their first paid job through interactive strategies.

2. The Client

The client is usually referred to as an organization or

individual who employs the services of a digital marketer. It is an official name for a customer, but for the sake of classification, a client is any organization or individual that needs the services that a digital marketer provides. The client is the most sought-after party by the digital marketer due to the high competition in the market. The digital marketer is looking to make money by offering his services to his clients, and the clients, in turn, expect to get maximum value for their money in return in terms of quality and affordable services.

There's a high level of interaction between a digital marketer and a client due to their interdependence on one another. Every D.M has it at the back of his mind that there are fewer clients out there being chased by thousands of digital marketers who will readily offer the same services as you. In my years of seeking and interacting with clients from different industries, I learned that most clients have various options open to them to choose from. They like to be independent of your bargaining power and are devilishly attracted to low pricing. Therefore, their interaction with you is like an interaction between a man wooing a lady and is not mutual until you have fully gained their trust and developed a strong working relationship with them. It is important for you to carry out research about your potential clients and get a prior knowledge of their products or services. This will help you in your interaction with them and give you a heads-up on how to tailor your services to their needs. Otherwise, you are in a blind spot.

3. The Target Markets

The target market-digital market interaction is a non-formal interaction. The target market can be either a client or a customer, depending on the occasion. I was having a lot of confusion too, but every organization, even before producing a product, has a particular set of people that they are making the products specifically for. This implies that the target market is potential customers.

These potential customers are classified based on their geographical location, age, taste, and so many other demographics. The identification of the target market is borne out of the interaction between the D.M or D.M.A and the client. Before you are able to carry out or implement a marketing plan for a client, you have to identify the target market. This is information that your client will share with you upon agreement to work for them since they hold the true signature of their product and content.

4. The Item Or Services

The products and services are the property of the client, and your marketing plan is targeted at putting those products in front of the thousands of target customers. The product could be a pharmaceutical product, technology, software, cosmetics, fashion, or jewelry. On the other hand, the services might include consultancy services, B2B services, counseling and any other services. The D. M's goal is to push the company's products and services as much as the budget allows.

Having studied the activities of the aforementioned elements, I have been able to classify their interactions into the following:

- Client-Digital Marketer Interaction
- Client-Digital Marketer-Product Interaction
- Interaction with Customers

1. CLIENT-DIGITAL MARKETER INTERACTION

The client-digital market interaction is the first phase of interaction. It is simply the stage where the digital marketer meets the client. This stage is characterized by understanding the client's requirements, the introduction of the digital marketer, and analysis of the client's marketing objectives and budgeting.

2. CLIENT-DIGITAL MARKETER-PRODUCT INTERACTION

This stage is the introduction of the product. The interaction here is centered on the branding of the product, understanding the literature of the product, and who it is meant for. Here, the digital marketer gets a clear picture of the objectives of marketing that particular product. It's at this stage that the digital marketer shows his creative abilities. Some products might not have a good brand. The digital marketer might advise a rebranding of the product.

3. INTERACTION WITH CUSTOMERS

This is the final stage of interaction, and it's a non-formal interaction. The digital marketer would have gathered enough data from the Client-Digital Marketer Interaction stage to form a knowledgeable opinion about who the product is meant for and the strategies to reach them.

These interactive strategies are the bridge that connects the digital marketer and the client, and they include the following:

- *Interact Traditionally:*

Digital marketers need to understand the importance of using traditional interactions to reach their clients. Finding a client for your digital agency should not depend solely on the digital world. The same way every service provider seeks out clients is the same way a digital marketer seeks out clients.

This can happen by building a strong relationship with the clients by connecting with them at local events where business owners and decision-makers are where the crowd is. They are attracted to events that will put them in front of their customers. These might include trade fairs, seminars, vocational centers, and meetings. At these events, you'll get the chance to formally introduce yourself to these companies who are present at the events and demonstrate to them first-hand how your services can change their business. The digital marketer needs to understand that all these interactions are what build up into a digital marketer-client relationship that can translate into future business between the two. This allows you to build your list of potential clients, have a knowledge of the local businesses and what they do, and so you can be able to understand the possible problems they face and how to offer solutions to them.

In my own words, local businesses are the core ingredients that every start-up or newcomer needs and are foundational to their growth. The social culture of capturing your local business clients helps you to grow from there and expand your tentacles easily. However, before engaging in such interactions, there are some things that you need to put in place, which will be looked at in chapter ten of this book, 'Be your own client'.

Business is simply the politics of exchange and leverage. What can you do for me and how do I return the favour? Once you have established the presence of those businesses, refer people to the businesses. These businesses will definitely complete the interaction, and there's a high possibility they will be converted to become your clients or return the favour and refer others to your business. The right conference can be a game-changer for your business. If you are keen to learn how in detail, here is Vanessa Van Edwards, Behavioral Investigator, explaining more:

1. Create Online Directories

The Internet, they say, is the most powerful research tool in the hand of the right user. So many people underestimate the use of the internet when they are looking for answers. Gathering online directories is one of the best strategies a digital marketer can use to increase his client's database by using either Google, Yelp, or many other search engines on the internet. But if these searches aren't narrowed down to a specific category such as digital agency directories, these allow you to search for the right categories and the results are likely that everyone on the directory is looking for the services you provide.

"Shadows do not reflect your bad images; it is only misjudged because you decided to stand against the light."
— **ADENEKAN MAYOWA ADEBAYO**

SUMMARY

This gives an insight into some of the fallacious beliefs about digital marketing and pointedly stress the needs to be passionate about one's career pursuits. The real drivers of a digital marketer are burning desire to learn, grow and change in the ever-evolving digital world. When the passion for your career is powerful, failure will only make you stronger.

Be a Digital Marketing Rockstar

2

CUSTOMER AVATAR
Describe your ideal customer age, location, lifestyle, profession, pains, gains, and what social media they are using

1

CUSTOMER JOURNEY
Map out a buying process that you believe your avatar will easily follow. Create a journey that will provide value and awakens curiosity

3

FREE & PAID TRAFFIC
Plan a strategy to introduce yourself to your avatar social media ads & posts. Use videos and affiliate programs. Use SEO and key buzz words. Plan for multi devices activity.

4

WEB CONTENT PLAN
Write blog posts that educate your avatar about why, how and what you do that gives value to your clients. Your avatar is coming to life = a lead.

6

AUTOMATIC EMAIL MARKETING, SMS & RETARGETING ADS
Segment your leads and keep in touch with automation. Follow up & provide value to support their journey.

5

OPT-IN FORMS
Offer your leads the opportunity to receive more value. Through registration forms they can access white papers, video training, demos, trial period, members area.

7

CONVERSION
When your leads trust you and believe that you can help them solve their problem or need, they will buy from you.

8

DELIVER & WOW
Go that extra mile with your new customer and you will most likely have a new ambassador referring new leads to you.

CHAPTER SIX

A TRUE DIGITAL MARKETER

In my years in the digital space, there isn't one day I have ever developed a doubt about my choice of career. Perhaps it is one of the reasons why I have developed a thick skin against stiff competition in the business. There are so many people who have taken up digital marketing as a means of making quick money to survive an economic downturn or because they have lost their job. If you are one of those types of people, then the digital space is not for you because such people are a class of people who are volatile, poignant, and don't have the threshold of patience to wait for the slow-paced income of digital marketing to convert. Yes, digital marketing requires a lot of patience and hard work.

So, I'm sure you're wondering, "How do I develop myself into a true digital marketer, focus, and turn around perspective?" It's not farfetched. First you need to discover the true qualities of a digital marketer, not just any stereotyped digital skills, but the ones inherent to you as a pioneering digital marketer.

What makes you a true digital marketer and sets you apart from the others?

- *Your ability to maintain consistency:*

Most beginners are dead on arrival due to a lack of patience on their journey into digital marketing. Research has it that most businesses suffer losses in the first six months of start-up and only experience profits in the second year of the business. The same thing applies to digital marketing; the first year of venturing into the industry, either as an individual marketer or as a digital marketing agency, is usually the roughest and also the moment you get to learn a lot about the prospects of your business. To know what you did right or what you need to do to improve. Typically, most use it to build a good name for their brand or agency rather than make money.

But unfortunately, most beginners give up even before their efforts start to yield results, and then hit rock-bottom and start all over again. They find themselves in a loop because of the inability to start and complete a project, almost like you're running in circles and afraid of getting into the game of competition.

Starting up in December, 2016, I faced the same problem. I would start a campaign and cancel the projects every week, wasting resources, time, and money. I began to make comparisons and question my methods. I discovered that I had no business identity due to my lack of consistency and was too afraid to follow through on a project for fear of failure. Since it was a self-financed campaign, I took the time to experiment and test the waters, and within a few weeks, I began to experience my consistency:

- It encourages trust between the brand and the audience.
- It gives a feeling of stability to your customers.
- It helps customers recognize and remember your brand.

I was already determined to follow through with the

process whether I made a profit or not. I was more focused on the bigger picture: to grow, learn, and evolve with the process.

- *Ability to adapt to changes in the market.*

The industry changes every day due to consumer behavior, new brands, and changes in technology. A digital marketer is faced with the task of marketing different brands or products for a client. They wear different hats every day. So, therefore, what worked for PZ Global Services, whose flag product is toothpaste, might not work for Nature Fresh, a cosmetic producing firm whose flag product is a beauty cream. It is your ability to analyze the consumer behavior of your target audience and adopt the reigning technological know-how that will allow you to come up with a marketing strategy specifically tailored towards your next target market.

- *Your ability to use available resources to meet your goals.*

Once you land your first gig, your client will definitely have a budget for the type of marketing services you intend to provide. As a digital marketer, you should be able to set a threshold on the amount you want to spend on social media advertising and SEO. By setting a target, you will be able to meet the spending requirements of your client and achieve your desired milestone.

- *Your ability to distinguish between facts and fallacies is dependent on your*

There are so many fallacies about digital marketing that a true digital marketer should be able to differentiate them from the facts in order to make good judgment calls in this line of career. Some of this fallacy includes:

Social media is inexpensive.

False. As Charlene Li has stated, social media exchanges media costs for labor costs. When done correctly, social media — even a simple track record monitoring program — is a time-consuming proposition that necessitates constant monitoring.

Social media is a quick way to communicate.

False. By definition, social media is sluggish. When

done right, social media is about building genuine interactions with consumers and prospects in their natural environment. That is not a "wave the magic wand" situation. You must develop content, participate in several communities, and work in little steps. Many influential programs take months (or even years) to sprout.

Social Media is "Viral Marketing."

In the same way that a square is also a rectangle, a rectangle isn't a square. Can a social media program go viral? Absolutely. But if you're engaged in a social media program in an effort to go "viral," you're not really engaged in social media at all. You're engaged in an advertising and marketing campaign that uses the Web as its distribution platform.

Results from social media can't be measured.

False. As compared to many other communication initiatives, such as traditional PR, TV advertising, outdoor advertising, and so on, social media really provides quite good analytics. Many social media software packages can generate extremely detailed reports on the effectiveness of social media programs. Can such findings be linked directly to sales and, hence, ROI? Probably not yet, but where OTHER than search and email (and possibly banners) can you do it?

Use of social media is optional.

It makes no difference what your consumers' demographics are. It makes no difference what industry you work in. Customers and prospects are talking about you on the internet. Your firm must be a part of that discussion. Today, many people do their talking online, so that's where you need to be. If barbershops still influenced customer attitude, I'd be writing this piece about barbershop marketing. Be present where your clients are.

Social media is difficult.

False. It's not difficult; it's convoluted. That is all due to the alphabet soup of social networks, livestreams, sharing sites, and so on. Social media isn't only about Facebook, Myspace, Flickr, Twitter, blogs, or YouTube. It is about developing a strategy to transform your company or organization into more of a human being and less of a machine. It is all about humanization. Customers and prospects will want to be a part of your firm if they believe it is more human and cares about them. That is the holy grail of brand involvement that we are all looking for. Humanization occurs far too frequently.

- *Your ability to translate your research into a competitive advantage.*

A true digital marketer must possess the skills of translating research into data that will make his strategy successful. This comes in handy when analyzing campaign data and translating customer interactions with the product or service in order to adjust and deliver tailored content at every step of the customer's online journey. This requires the digital marketer to learn some Google analytical skills too.

"Customers are like car drivers that branch in and out of a roundabout, your job is to nurture them and make sure you keep them within your circle always."
— **ADENEKAN MAYOWA ADEBAYO**

SUMMARY

Digital Marketers need to understand that as much as they seek to get new customers for a company, they shouldn't forget to nurture the already existing ones, by understanding their journey, strategizing ways to encourage them to remain your loyal customers.

The Digital Marketing Circle

CHAPTER SEVEN

DIGITAL MARKETING CIRCLE

Curiosity, they say, can lead one to undiscovered treasures of knowledge. Being curious was one of the many traits I have developed that have helped me a lot during research. I always wondered about how customers find certain products online and why that particular product was in high demand until I was introduced into the world of digital marketing. I would ask questions like, "Did the owner just put them on the internet and the buyers just stumble on them by chance while surfing the internet?" Where and how did they get those products, and why are they more popular than others?

The network of events in the digital marketing world can be very confusing. The digital marketing circle breaks this down into phases of interconnected activities so that even a newbie can be able to understand the events that lead to a direct sale or generating customers online for a client, even if their business is offline. The journey of a customer in digital marketing is of high importance, as this will help the DM know what, where, and how a customer ends up buying a product and what things need to be in place while waiting for the arrival of the customer (king). The term "Digital Marketing Circle" refers to a series of repetitive activities that describe a customer's journey from following social platforms to visiting a website and eventually purchasing a product or subscribing to a service.

Therefore, a digital marketing circle simply refers to the customer's journey from point A to point B, and then from B to A again, where point A to point B represents the entire activities of the campaign. Unlike a digital marketing campaign that comes to an end, a digital marketing circle does not end. The knowledge the DM learns from initiating the process goes back into the circle and it continues to improve it. Such knowledge comes from observing a digital marketing sales funnel, then replicating it into a circle of continuous activities. It, however, varies from customer to customer.

Basically, it involves the following, though it might differ due to its relativity to the objectives of each campaign. But typically, according to Nigel Temple, the digital marketing circle involves the following steps:

Circle of Digital Marketing

1. PROFILING:

Every digital marketer needs prior research about the target market for their campaign. Profiling will help them understand how the target market behaves, where to find them, how to reach them and what their interests are. So, one can be able to record and analyze their behavioral characteristics in order to have some degree of predictability in terms of their buying power, their usage of similar products, and their preferences. This will help you as a digital marketer to narrow them down according to the purpose of your campaign. For instance, Huggrant Manufacturing Company, who produces

2. KEYWORDS

Here, the keywords refer to SEO keywords that your potential customers use when they search for your product or services on any search engine. SEO is a vital part of the Circle of Digital Marketing. This comes to show that it is a continuous process, as one keyword that might generate a lot of leads today might not be so active in a couple of months. There's a need to optimize the website's SEO content, whether on the client's website or on other platforms.

3. WEB COPY

According to Nigel's concept, great content should follow after creating SEO for your website. The contents have to be interesting to keep the visitors busy. The content should also be in line with the niche of the website so it can give a reader an impression that such services are available.

4. SOCIAL MEDIA

Digital marketers should learn to also apply synergy by taking advantage of other digital marketing platforms such as Facebook, Twitter, and Instagram.

- Learn from your customers and improve upon their feedback about your products.
- Landing Page

The landing page is where your potential customers will go once, they follow the link from your various channels. It could be a website landing page to subscribe to a service or a page to download an app. So, it is important that you make a good first impression in order to keep the customer.

Why do you need to understand the Digital Marketing Circle?

- The Digital Marketing Circle helps you understand the flow of events that occur after a campaign is launched.
- To help you, have a glimpse into the journey of the customer and adjust your campaign accordingly to their interactions with your marketing channels.
- The digital marketing circle is a long-term marketing strategy that aims to retain existing customers while also acquiring new ones.
- It is ideal for promoting an entire company with similar services.

A Digital Marketing Funnel:

What is a digital marketing funnel?

Digital Marketing Funnel is simply Digital Marketing in practice. By definition, it is a strategic model created by the digital marketer to pinpoint the journey of a potential customer with the intention of buying and to the time they take action to buy and become a customer. This concept is basically all about segmenting the communication actions of the buyer.

The information gathered from a digital marketing funnel is what feeds the digital marketing circle and improves the continuity of good marketing practice. By adopting the knowledge gathered from the Digital Marketing funnel into the circle, customers get better services tailored to their needs.

Stages of Digital Marketing Funnels

There are numerous digital marketing funnels because each DM creates his own strategy to suit his campaign. But basically, the stages of the digital marketing funnel include the following:

- Exposure
- Discovery
- Consideration
- Conversion
- Customer Relationship
- Retention

Why is it so important to your strategy?

In practice, why is the funnel concept so crucial in any digital marketing strategy?

- It is important to make the customer's journey a thrilling experience, meeting their expectations every step of the way by directing quality content and ads that are crucial for the buyer's journey. For example, a buyer who follows a lead from a Facebook ad about a new technology to a website should see a great landing page, quality content (description of the product, followed by the price, and then a buy or order button). That way, the customer would not be misled by unnecessary information or taken directly to a page without enlightening the buyer of what they want to buy.

- In cases where the DM has a sales team in place to handle the final conversation, it makes the job easier as the buyer is led to the sales team.
- If the concept of the digital marketing funnel is applied well, it brings the brand close to the buyer and makes them more relevant in the course of buying.
- This concept tends to increase the productivity of your whole marketing team. Knowing the journey of the buyer, your team is mandated to create content as needed to improve the customer's journey.
- Breaking down the journey into segments makes it possible for the DM to communicate with the right audience and offer tailored content.
- Having knowledge of the Digital Marketing Funnel helps the DM to encourage the buyers to move to the next stage.

How to Create Your Own Digital Marketing Funnel

Creating a digital marketing funnel is an important part

of your strategy, and not every DM is skilled enough to be able to achieve it or know how to go about it.

Step I

Goal setting for your actions

You need to know whether your goal is to increase sales, or to upsell, increase return on investment (ROI), get better leads, or increase brand awareness.

Step II

In this step, you need to design your funnel. It's best to often make reference to an already existing homogenous sales funnel to create one for your business or brand. In this step, you have to specify the part that incorporates your sales cycle.

Step III

In this step, all you need to do is spell out the things you need to do to make each step enjoy traffic. For instance, in the following stages of the sales cycle, it is your job to generate enough traffic to each through emails, phone calls, or face-to-face meetings.

Understanding the Flow of Digital Marketing Funnels

The Digital Marketing Funnel will model the various actions points and map out the buyer's journey. Your job as the DM is to understand the marketing funnel you have adopted as your marketing strategy and make better use of the resources at your disposal.

Understanding how the digital marketing funnel works will ensure that your actions are more accurate, making better use of your company's available resources and impacting users who may become consumers of your brand.

That's why we separated the best types of content for each stage. Check it out!

According to webFX, there are three types of digital marketing funnels, including

- Digital marketing funnel in the shape of an hourglass
- Looping Digital Marketing Funnel
- Digital Marketing Funnel for Micro Moments

"There's a bit of anything in everything, a bit of old things in new things and a bit of everything is anything. Do not shut yourself up, be open to ideas, accepting both sides."
— ADENEKAN MAYOWA ADEBAYO

SUMMARY

Most digital marketers have embraced the new technology and neglected the traditional marketing that rooted Digital Marketing. This chapter traces the importance of mixing the two, adopting them in your marketing strategies.

CHAPTER EIGHT

DIGITAL MARKETING WITH TRADITIONAL RULES

I grew up in the 80s and it was the era that appreciated newspapers, magazines, radio, and television as a means of communication between businesses and their target audience. Most businesses get their products featured in magazines by paying for pages just to advertise their products. One would encounter adverts in magazines from popular brands such as Seven-up, Bourn Vita, and other fashion brands such as Dolce & Gabbana. Also, TVs usually show advertisements when showing a drama or interesting program. These ads do not take more than five to six minutes. It gets to a point where it becomes too frequent. Adverts come up every ten minutes into the show and it starts to get boring. Most people abandon the program because it has been littered with too many irrelevant commercials. They are too frequent and eat up valuable time from the TV show. I had no idea that what I had witnessed growing up was traditional marketing at its best.

The Digital Marketing industry's growth took shape around 2012 and 2018. The growth was tagged at around 25% to 40% yearly. The use of mobile apps, websites, and emails grew tremendously across the globe and introduced the era of digital marketing.

According to research by Expert Market Research, the global digital marketing market reached a value of nearly USD 305 billion in 2020. They posit that the market will grow at a CAGR of 17.6% between 2021 and 2026. Factors on which these predictions were based include an increase in people consuming and creating content through digital platforms.

A lot of digital marketers plunge into confusion when it comes to deciding which marketing strategy to choose, whether it be traditional marketing or digital marketing. Some even go as far as terming one contemporary and the other an old and archaic form of marketing. There is no doubt that there are still some levels of traditional marketing in digital marketing strategies. Some organizations still practice traditional marketing and it still works for them. So, what exactly is traditional marketing?

Traditional marketing is the use of traditional means to reach the audience such as billboards, TV, and newspapers (known as print media) as opposed to Kotler and Armstrong's (2019) definition of marketing, which says: *"Marketing is the process by which companies create value for customers and build strong customer relationships in order to capture value from customers in return."* Therefore, the only difference between the two types of marketing is the medium through which the customer is reached.

Digital Marketing And Traditional Marketing:

What makes digital marketing and traditional marketing essentially different is the medium through which they pass their marketing message to their targeted audience. Traditional marketing makes use of traditional media like newspapers, magazines, radio, and TV, while digital marketing uses digital media, such as social media (Facebook, Instagram, Twitter, YouTube), or websites. Due to the growth of digital platforms and its adaptations to business, hence the rising need for digital marketing, many are of the opinion that digital marketing is old fashion, but that's not true. There is still some level of traditional marketing in digital marketing.

Traditional marketing plays an important role that digital marketing does not, by establishing physical interactions through word-of-mouth advertising, which is missing in most advertising strategies. This is particularly important in situations where the customer has a need to meet with the people behind a particular brand. Stepping out of the digital world becomes necessary.

Furthermore, people still read magazines and newspapers even though digitalization has made it easy to gain access to a lot of things online with just a few clicks away. Newspapers and magazines are focused on a particular niche with genuine content tailored to your taste and are easy to read. Unlike searching for a fashion product online, Google will feed you with a lot of options according to your search. Filtering the information is entirely up to you.

In the same vein, digital marketing is also important, just like traditional marketing, though some will argue that it is the best type of marketing so far. Digital marketing incorporates every action you take while surfing or using the internet to create the best method of reaching you.

For example, you might be googling a type of cooking recipe in Nigeria or an international dish, and there's a chance that you might start seeing about the nearest restaurants specifically tailored to your search. Digital marketing just uses this to its advantage by cleverly weaving marketing communications into every digital channel.

Which Type Of Marketing Should You Use?

The key to a successful marketing strategy is striking the correct mix between conventional and digital channels. Digital marketing is the yin to conventional marketing's yang in 2020. Both are crucial components of a marketing plan, but they are enhanced when utilized in tandem. Take, for example, Guiness. Their TV ads are well-known for their distinctive and striking cinematography. Guinness' famous 1999 "Surfer" campaign is considered one of the finest TV advertisements of all time, even after more than 25 years. Despite its legendary position, Guinness must keep up with the changes and include digital marketing in their plans in order to avoid missing out on some enormous marketing possibilities.

Traditional Marketing: Advantages And Disadvantages

Traditional marketing is sometimes devalued by marketers due to the emergence of social media. Traditional marketing, on the other hand, has a place in a consumer's day-to-day existence. If you have the resources to promote your initiatives in publications and on prime-time television, your money might be well spent.

- Traditional marketing channels include:
- Outdoor (billboards, bus/taxi wraps, posters etc.)
- Broadcasting (TV, radio, etc.)
- Print (magazines, newspapers, etc.)
- Direct Mail (catalogues etc.)
- Telemarketing (Phone, text message)
- Window display and signs

Advantages:

Effective and simple to grasp.

A visually appealing billboard or a captivating TV ad is a common occurrence in most people's daily lives. They're simple to understand and frequently funny.

Printed marketing materials are more long-lasting.

If you place an ad in The New York Times, it will remain until the magazine is recycled.

That's fantastic if the customer is a collector.

More enduring

Seeing something in person rather than on your phone increases the likelihood of remembering it. The anticipation of new Super Bowl commercials or a magnificent and striking window display is more likely to stick with you than an Instagram ad you'll likely swipe through in seconds.

Disadvantages:

Campaigns are more difficult to measure.

Traditional marketing efforts can be measured using

tools such as brand trackers, but they are nowhere near as in-depth or clever as the methods available for digital marketing.

Frequently costly.

If you're a new brand, chances are you don't have the budget for a four-page spread in Vogue. Many types of conventional marketing will cost you a lot of money.

There is no direct interaction with the consumer.

Unlike social media marketing, you are largely unaware of your audience's reaction to your marketing efforts.

Digital marketing: Advantages and Disadvantages

"Internet users now account for 57 percent of the worldwide population," according to Click Z. People spend an average of 6 hours and 42 minutes every day online. By 2021, it is expected that mobile will account for 73% of all e-commerce sales. "

That's an insanely large amount of time and a chance to perform some effective internet marketing. Check out

Vistaprint's Digital Marketing Guide for Small Businesses for advice on developing an effective digital marketing plan.

Social media is one example of a digital marketing channel (Facebook, Instagram, etc.):

- Promotion of Website Content
- Marketing through affiliates
- Inbound marketing
- Marketing via email
- Pay-per-click (PPC)
- SEM (Search engine marketing)

The Advantages of Digital Marketing

More ways to participate

You can directly see what your customers think of your brand and marketing activities through platforms such as social media. If your campaign is being shared, liked, and receiving a lot of good feedback, you know you're doing something right.

It is simple to measure your campaigns.

In contrast to conventional marketing, the nuances of

digital marketing tracking are quite detailed. This clarifies your learning for your next round of marketing initiatives.

It allows for more precise aiming.

If you have the means to specifically target a 29-year-old female writer who likes Lizzo and Guinness, can't you also generate perfectly personalized content?

Digital Marketing's Drawbacks

Digital advertisements might be considered obnoxious.

Consider the following scenario: you're reading through your Facebook site and all you want to know is what your old school buddies are up to these days. Then you receive the terrible sponsored ad for anything connected to that embarrassing disease you looked up the night before. It's almost certain to make you actually despise the brand that's conducting the sophisticated targeting.

Less long-term

Digital marketing efforts like Google advertisements, banners, promotional emails, and social network ads can have a fleeting, transitory nature. They are intangible and readily overlooked. Your ad will be removed from their screen if they continue to scroll or click to the next page.

It is always changing.

There is a lot to understand in order to get the most out of your digital marketing efforts. From search engine marketing to social media, each channel usually requires its own specialist to get the most bang for your buck. A grassroots social media marketing approach, on the other hand, is a terrific place to start.

The Transition from Traditional to Digital Media Is Already Underway.

Digital, which was once an emerging space for brands and retailers to connect with tech-savvy consumers, has now become central to their lives. As consumers live more digitally, nearly every aspect of the human experience has migrated online.

Lives that are laser-focused Consumers are not only spending more time online, but they are also spending a larger portion of their money online. By 2020, consumers will have shifted 5% of their spending from brick and mortar to e-commerce.

Taking note of these consumer trends, marketers shifted their focus to digital in order to be present where consumers spend their time and money. By 2019, an inflection point had been reached, with digital marketing overtaking traditional forms of marketing spending in the US.

Unsurprisingly, forward-thinking businesses and industries were well ahead of this trend.

According to one marketing executive, *"In 2017, direct mail was completely removed from our budget—it wasn't even a tool in our toolkit."* We didn't get any pushback because we were looking for a higher ROI.

While some companies are ahead of the digital acceleration curve, marketing allocation remains a puzzle for businesses to solve. There is a constant need to reassess the relationship between digital and traditional media in order to create the most effective media mix to achieve business objectives.

If you haven't made the switch yet, here's what you're missing.

Because digital is so effective at moving people along the customer journey, it has emerged as the dominant form of marketing spend. In fact, digital marketing is 24 percent more likely to drive cross-channel engagement (visits to social media, websites, and in-store).

While Traditional Has Its Place, The Future Is Digital.

The value of traditional mail marketing has high points within specific customer segments. Among these customer segments, older consumers (57+) are 48 percent more likely to prefer traditional mail to digital marketing. Not only do older consumers prefer traditional mail, but they are also a valuable segment, accounting for the majority of top-spending customers in many industries that continue to rely heavily on traditional mail. "The audience that responds to direct mail channels is shrinking, but it is still there," a marketing mix subject matter expert explained.

While older consumers may prefer traditional, this is not true for all key consumer segments, so companies must balance traditional and digital media formats.

"You do not need to quench my success for yours to shine brighter, together we can shine even brighter."
— **ADENEKAN MAYOWA ADEBAYO**

SUMMARY

The Author explains the need to work as a team to achieve a task, as it will be a lot easier, cheaper and more efficient to work as a team. Understanding the limitations that the ignorance of this fact may cause is very important in Digital Marketing. Every project demands a project team, and the success of the project depends on their power of collective initiatives.

DIGITAL MARKETING IN 5 STEPS

Digital marketing can be confusing, but understand the process is simple and repeatable. Start your successful digital marketing campaign with these five steps.

1 Define a target audience

It's impossible to hit a target blindfolded and with both arms tied behind your back. Creating marketing campaigns without your target audience is no different. Understanding your audience is necessary for making a connection.

2 Create remarkable content

With your target audience in sight. It's time to focus on creating content of interest to them. Creating remarkable content is the hook that captures your audience's attention

3 Build an email list

Even the most receptive audience may not have the time or budget to do business with you today. Overcome these hurdles by building an email list you can nurture until your audience is in better standing.

4 Make sales

The best products and services still need a show of emotion to satisfy your customer's needs. If great content is the engine driving your digital marketing machine, then sales are where the rubber meets the road.

5 Measure, optimize & repeat

Digital marketing makes measurement easy and affordable. Analyzation allows you to gain helpful insight when optimizing your targeting, content, and sales processes. For the best results, repeat to keep growing your business.

CHAPTER NINE

FIRM AND INDIVIDUAL SYNERGY AND COLLECTIVE INITIATIVE POWER

I remember using that word "synergy" countless times during my presentations and prep talks at university when I was talking about team play and the need to come together and utilize knowledge to achieve something greater.

Though in most texts I've read, profit-making organizations have attached profit as the end product of synergy. It's why the word is a common terminology in merger and acquisition. But as I grew in the field of Digital Marketing, I came to realize that synergy could be applied in marketing, not just as a collaborative human effort but as the utilization of multiple marketing channels to meet our marketing goals and objectives.

Synergy Between A DM And His Agency:

This synergy happens when a digital marketer works for an agency and is required to carry out day-to-day digital marketing responsibilities. This synergy will help the DM fit into any team he might encounter in the agency. It could be a project that needs a digital marketer. For example, the management team of an artist needs a digital marketer who understands what it means to work as a team.

Synergy of Using Multiple Marketing Channels

A campaign that was run with just one marketing channel has fewer chances of meeting its milestone than a campaign that was promoted using multiple marketing channels. These channels include promoting via your website, e-newsletter, social media pages (Facebook, Twitter, and Instagram), and Google AdWords.

Advantages:

- *An Increase in Brand Awareness:*

Using more than one marketing channel provides a shortfall in case one channel fails; the others will be used to reach the targeted milestone of the campaign. This reduces the risk of relying on one channel. For example, a customer who saw an advertisement for a Digital Marketing masterclass on Facebook may be persuaded to act if he sees the same advertisement on Google Display campaign. This will gradually begin to sow in their minds as more of the advert is repeated on different channels.

- *Broader Coverage of the Target Customers:*

Online Marketing Synergy makes it easy to cover a wider scope of your target market by exploring multiple marketing channels for your campaign. If your digital marketing campaign only uses one channel, it limits your reach and coverage. because some of the target customers may prefer Facebook while others prefer Twitter and YouTube

- *Credibility—credibility in business is everything.*

A customer buys a product that they trust or have knowledge of. Consumers are cautious when it comes to online purchases due to the increase in the amount of digital misrepresentation of products where a product does not match what was displayed in the ad description. Consumers have various options to choose from.

Typically, people who buy products online behave in this manner.

The consumer carries out research on the product or services. Compare the products with a close substitute identifying the product according to their needs.

The above illustration shows that customers spend a lot of time in the funnel before making a decision to buy. Doing so, they encounter so many marketing channels as they carry out their own research. The synergy of using multiple channels will repeatedly put your products in front of the customer when he submits your products to a search engine to make enquiries or to compare them with other similar products or services.

With the above behavior, it is clear that the consumer is a rational-thinking consumer that likes to understand what they are buying by carrying out research on their items of need in a bid to find the best options available to them. In the course of that, products or companies that have adopted online marketing synergy are at a great advantage.

Finding A Balance: Between Digital and Traditional Marketing Synergy

Digital marketing (also known as "modern marketing") is a type of marketing in which services and products are promoted using online and internet-based technologies, platforms, and channels. Traditional marketing promotes services and products through non-digital channels, the four most common of which are print, broadcast, telephone, and direct mail.

Small business owners must recognize that traditional marketing still has a place in any effective business strategy as the world becomes more digital-first. A healthy mix of digital and non-digital marketing efforts is the most effective way for startups and small businesses to grow. And so, while striking the ideal balance between digital and traditional marketing efforts may appear difficult, it is entirely within your grasp.

The Most Important Digital Channels for a Successful Marketing Strategy

Businesses can now reach more consumers than ever before thanks to the advancement of all things digital. However, simply putting your business online does not guarantee more customers, higher sales, or greater profitability. You'll still need to put in some effort! Here are a few examples of digital channels that can be used as part of an effective marketing strategy:

Business website:

Your website serves as your small business's digital storefront. When used correctly, it aids in the capture of new leads, the conversion of potential customers, and the retention of existing customers. However, the sooner you realize that your website will never be finished, the better off you will be.

Sites for social networking

Effective social media marketing necessitates knowing who your target demographic is, which social platforms they use, and how to best appeal to them on each. Conduct some social listening to learn what your target audience wants most from your brand or industry, and then tailor your social strategy to meet those needs. Don't forget about social media advertising, either!

Google My Business Listing:

So, you've put your company online. You've optimized your website, set up your social media accounts, and are ready to start bringing in customers. The next step is to ensure that your customers can find you through a simple Google search. A well-optimized Google My Business listing ensures that your company appears in local business searches. It also increases brand visibility and establishes rapport with potential customers.

Email Marketing:

With an average return on investment of $42 for every dollar spent on email marketing, incorporating this medium into your digital marketing strategy is a no-brainer. A solid email marketing strategy converts leads into customers and first-time buyers into repeat customers.

Self-promotion often comes as one of the most difficult things to do by business owners or brands. In my own opinion, the marketing should start with you. Often times, Digital Marketing always wonder the internet searching for ways to land their first gig with a multi-national company and neglect the tool which is at their disposal. Some might say, they do not have the finance to sponsor a viral campaign but forget about organic traffic. The same way you are searching for ways to increase your patronage is the same ways business who need your services are searching for your services online. Therefore, taking time to brand your business, optimizing it on google and social media platforms, getting a blog or website would go a long way in putting your services in front of clients online.

"We are our first customers, a complete reflection of our services in self-advertisement of what the world will expect us to offer them when they decide to patronize us."
— **ADENEKAN MAYOWA ADEBAYO**

SUMMARY

The author designed this chapter for personal growth. Branding, SEO, getting a website, content creation of your own business is important not just to help you get organized, self-advertise but it also gives your client an insight about the type of services they will expect.

Steps To Social Media Marketing Success

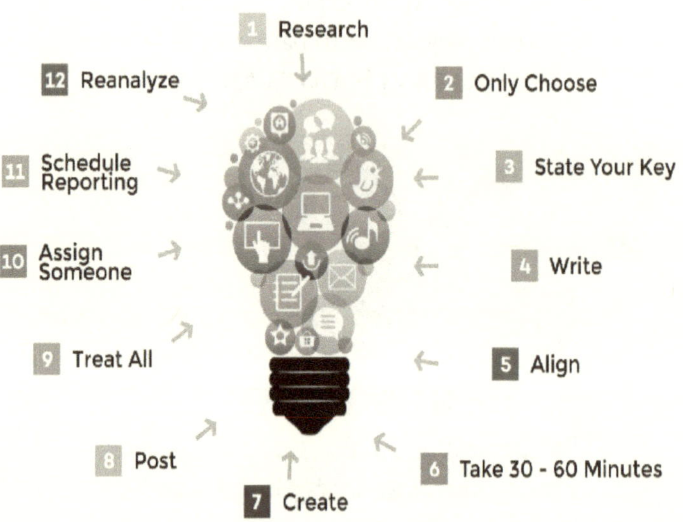
1 Research
12 Reanalyze
2 Only Choose
11 Schedule Reporting
3 State Your Key
10 Assign Someone
4 Write
9 Treat All
5 Align
8 Post
6 Take 30 - 60 Minutes
7 Create

CHAPTER TEN

BE YOUR OWN CLIENT

Branding Your Own Business

Why is it critical to brand your company?

Organizations of all sizes, regardless of size, must engage in branding in order to remain relevant. If you're still questioning why, you should brand your company, consider the following advantages.

1. Set your company apart from the competition.

With so many firms offering comparable services or goods, it can be difficult to distinguish them. This is where branding comes into play. Your beliefs, story, brand promise, and other assets allow you to demonstrate your distinctiveness. Using these to establish a point of distinction might help you stand out from the crowd.

2. To become more well-known

Another advantage of investing in a regular branding effort is that your brand will become more memorable. Customers get more familiar with your organization when they can recognize it based on physical, visual, and audio cues. This fosters trust, which 81% of customers rely on when making a purchasing decision. Customers' memories and engagement with your content, emails, or advertisements may also be influenced by brand awareness.

3. Build client loyalty.

Powerful brands frequently have a devoted following, but this does not happen by happenstance. It arises from providing unique experiences and content to their viewers that they can relate to in order to establish a bond. You will have more consumers who will support your business and share their great experiences if you make an emotional connection with them. This edge might imply more repeat business, reduced churn, and more word-of-mouth recommendations.

How to Brand Your Company in 7 Easy Steps

So, how do you go about establishing a consistent personality and style for your company? Let's divide it into seven steps.

1. Determine your target audience.

In this case, you are looking at a business that will need your services as a digital marketer.

2. Develop your value proposition.

Your brand promise is your value proposition. It is more than a catchphrase or a slogan. A unique value proposition (UVP) illustrates how your product solves the challenges of your ideal clients better than rivals.

3. Establish your purpose and basic principles.

What is the purpose of your company? This question is addressed by your mission. To create an effective mission statement, define your company's purpose, who your customers are, the goods or services you provide, and how you do it. To make it easier to remember, summarize it in a few words. The following is an example of a mission statement.

4. Identify your brand's personality.

Your brand personality, like that of a human, is a conglomeration of attributes that your company possesses. Preferably, these attributes will appeal to consumers and form their impressions of your firm. As a result, having a personality that connects with your clients may help you develop an empathetic relationship and differentiate yourself from the competition.

Consider the attributes you want your brand to be associated with. Do you want to be known as an innovator, a capable leader, or a charismatic personality? Choose your characteristics and the voice you'll use to communicate. If your corporate image is rough, for example, your brand voice may be confident and forceful.

5. Develop brand assets.

The next stage is to select the pieces that will serve as your company's identity. Colors, typefaces, packaging, slogans, and your logo are a few examples. Certain colors elicit different emotions and communicate different ideas. According to the rules of branding, red increases vitality, yellow increases optimism, and purple stimulates the imagination.

Whatever logo, color scheme, and style you pick to identify your company, make sure it is distinct and easily identifiable. To generate ideas, consult with experts and your team, as well as experiment with logo creators (such as Looka).

6. Apply them to all of your channels.

Now that your branding elements are complete, disseminate them across all of your platforms. You may, for example, incorporate visual assets such as your logo, colors, and fonts throughout all of your communications. On the About Us page, a longer version of your goal statement might function as your brand story.

Although your basic beliefs will usually remain on your

website, branded films and articles can help consumers and future workers understand what you stand for. Keep in mind that branding is an ongoing activity that will last as long as your organization does.

7.Maintain consistency.

According to Marketing Nutz, it might take up to 5-7 brand impressions for a person to recall your brand. Branding must be consistent throughout all platforms, including the website, social media, and offline contact with customers. Create brand guidelines to increase cohesion.

Is your brand's voice on social media youthful and casual? Then you won't have to be stiff on your blogs. When your customers see your content, trademarks, or other brand assets, they should know what to expect or feel. Continuity fosters recognition, credibility, and commitment. These emotions are indicative of good branding.

Who Would Benefit from Digital Marketing Services?

A recent survey found that 70–80 percent of shoppers research a company online before visiting them in person or making a purchase. This means that firms that wish to be found by potential clients must have an internet presence.

If your company falls into this category of needing to improve its online presence, you should consider investing in digital marketing services. Digital marketing services may help your company get noticed, generate website visits, and attract more consumers than ever before.

What Do Digital Marketing Services Entail?

Digital marketing is a sort of marketing that involves the use of various tools, tactics, and strategies to boost a company's online presence. "Digital marketing" is often used as an umbrella term for services like social media marketing, search engine optimization (SEO), website construction, pay per click (PPC) advertising, and others.

Businesses frequently use digital marketing service providers to assist them in obtaining more followers, increasing website traffic, converting website visitors into leads, and attracting more consumers. Indeed, there are several advantages to investing in digital marketing services.

The Advantages of Digital Marketing Services

The advantages are numerous because digital marketing is a catch-all category for a wide range of internet marketing services. Finally, it comes down to the sorts of digital marketing services you use and your business goals.

The following are the most prevalent advantages of digital marketing:

Creating an appealing, professional-looking website

Increase your social media following and engagement by publishing compelling material on your website and blog.

- Increase consumer acquisition with sponsored advertising.
- Increasing your Google and Bing search engine rankings

- Increasing foot traffic and local search customers Improving your online conversion rate and marketing ROI
- Increasing the authority and exposure of your brand through public relations
- Increasing the number of high-authority, SEO-boosting backlinks to your website is a must.
- Investing in digital marketing services may assist a wide range of organizations. Continue reading to find out if digital marketing is ideal for your company.

Companies that want digital marketing services

Essentially, any business that wants to expand their internet presence and attract more clients may profit from digital marketing services. This is true for a rising number of organizations, as more people use the internet to discover the products and services they require.

With that in mind, these are the sorts of businesses that profit the most from digital marketing:

Automobile Dealerships

While auto dealerships draw foot visitors, they also earn a significant amount of business through internet searches. Local dealerships will want to appear in the search results if a potential consumer searches for "auto dealerships near me." Organic search, in particular, may assist car dealerships in attracting more clients through organic search.

Restaurants and pubs

Restaurants and bars, like auto dealerships, draw a lot of business from local searches. A potential customer may search for "best Italian restaurants" or "happy hour near me" and expect to get a list of possibilities. Restaurants and bars may outrank their competition and attract more consumers by using digital marketing.

Ecommerce

Ecommerce enterprises sell things online and are thus significantly reliant on website visitors. Digital marketing helps e-commerce firms build their social media platforms, increase online interaction, and drive traffic to their websites.

Hotels & Hospitality

Hotels keep in business by generating online and over-the-phone bookings from customers wishing to stay in their neighborhood. As a result, hotels and other hospitality businesses rely on local SEO to attract customers. SEO, paid advertising, and social media promotion may all assist these sorts of businesses in producing more bookings.

Law Firms

The legal niche is very competitive, making it difficult for law firms to be noticed if they do not have an efficient digital marketing plan. Law firms may increase traffic and clients to their websites by using SEO, content marketing, social media marketing, and other forms of online marketing.

Medical/Healthcare

The medical specialty, like the legal industry, is very

competitive, and providers use digital marketing to attract customers on a consistent basis.

Even well-known hospitals and clinics require digital marketing to be seen in local search results.

Contractors/Construction Firms

HVAC, plumbing, and construction industries, among others, require digital marketing services to compete in local search. If your rivals dominate the search results, you'll have a difficult time finding new positions month after month. If you fit into this group, you should develop a complete digital marketing plan.

Moving Services

Moving firms are extremely localized and rely on local SEO to get seen in local search results. Optimizing your website for localized keywords, providing user-friendly content, and optimizing your company's local listings are all part of this form of digital marketing. You'll also need digital marketing if you want to book additional moving tasks. Providers of Online Services

To gain from digital marketing, you do not need to have

a physical office. Online service providers, like any other business, use digital marketing to stay competitive, stand out online, and attract new consumers. Yes, even other marketing and SEO businesses require marketing services in order to consistently drive traffic and leads.

Retailers

As more merchants go to ecommerce (online selling), it's becoming increasingly necessary for businesses to have a strong online presence, even if they have a local location. SEO, PPC, social media marketing, and email marketing may assist stores in increasing foot traffic and online sales.

Local Companies

While we have previously mentioned a few local businesses, the fact is that most small businesses require digital marketing in order to compete. Local SEO, in particular, may assist firms in outranking their local competition and attracting new clients on a regular basis.

REFERENCES

- Lauterborn B (1990) New marketing litany: four Ps passé; C-Words take over. Advert Age 61 (41):26
- American Marketing Association (2013, July) Definition of marketing. https://www.ama.org/AboutAMA/Pages/Definition-of-Marketing.aspx. Accessed 31 July 2015
- Krishnamurthy S (2006) Contemporary research in e-marketing. Hershey: Idea Group Inc (IGI)
- Osterwalder A., Pigneu Y (2010) Business model generation: a handbook for visionaries. New Jersey: Wiley
- Doran GT (1981) There's a SMART way to write management's goals and objectives. Manag rev

70(11):35–36

- Shultz C, Holbrook M (1999) Marketing and the tragedy of the commons: a synthesis, commentary, and analysis for action. J Public Policy Marke 18(2): 218–229

- 4. Kotler P (1967) Marketing management: analysis, planning, and control. New Jersey: Pearson Prentice Hall

- Godin S (1999) Permission marketing: turning strangers into friends and friends into customers. New York: Shimon & Shuster

- Laudon KC, Traver CG (2012) E-Commerce 2012 (8th revised edition). Boston: Prentice Hall

- Korper, S., & Ellis, J. (2001). The E-Commerce Book: building the e-empire. San Diego:Academic Press

- Quirk eMarketing (2012) Online Marketing Essentials. Lardbucket. http://2012books.lardbucket.org/pdfs/online-marketing-essentials.pdf Accessed 31 July 2015

- 26. Jimenez R (2009) Conocer las redes de afiliados. In E. Sanagustín (Ed.) Del 1.0 al 2.0, Claves para entender el nuevo marketing. (pp. 90-101). Bubok Publishing.

https://app.box.com/shared/tgoujqjm72 Accessed 26 July 2015

- Statista (2015). Global market share of search engines 2015 Statistics. http://www.statista.com/statistics/216573/worldwide-market-share-of-search-engines/ Accessed 27 July 2015

- Google (n.d.) Search Engine Optimization Starter G u i d e . http://static.googleusercontent.com/media/www.google.com/es//webmasters/docs/search-engine-optimization-starter-guide.pdf Accessed 26 July 2015

- Aaker, D. (2013). The New CMO Imperative: Spanning Silos. Boston: Harvard Business Press.

- Achrol, R.S. and Kotler, P. (1999). Marketing in the networked economy. Journal of Marketing, 63, special issue, pp. 146-163.

- Akella, J., Gargi, N. and Mehrotra, T. (2015). Putting digital process innovation at the center of organizational change, Mckinsey Insights and Publications, July. Available from: http://www.mckinsey.com/insights/business_technol

ogy/putting_digital_process_innovation_at_the_cent er_of_organizational_change [accessed 30 July 2015].

- Analogbei, M., Canhoto, A., Dibb, S., Quinn, L. and Simkin, L. (2015). Is marketing in the digital era losing its magic? Proceedings for the Academy of Marketing Conference, Limerick, July 2015.
- Antioco, M. and Kleijnen, M. (2010). Consumer adoption of technological innovations; effects of psychological and functional barriers in a lack of content versus a presence of content situation. European Journal of Marketing, 44 (11-12), pp. 1700-1724.
- Arndt, J. (1985). On making marketing science more scientific: the role of orientations, paradigms, metaphors and problem solving. Journal of Marketing, 49 (3), pp. 11-23.
- Armstrong, A. and Hagel, J. (1996). The real value of on-line communities. Harvard Business Review, 74 (3), pp. 134-140.
- Assael, H. (2010). From Silos to Synergy: a fifty-year review of cross media research. Journal of Advertising Research, 51 (1), pp. 43-58.

- Ba, S. and Pavlou, P.A. (2002). Evidence of the effect of trust building technology in electronic markets: price premiums and buyer behaviour. MIS Quarterly, 25 (3), pp. 243-268.

- Bart, I., Shanker, V., Sultan, F. and Urban, G. (2005). Are the drivers and role of online trust the same for all websites and consumers? A large scale exploratory empirical study. Paper 17, MIT Sloan School of Management, Cambridge, MA. Available at http://ebusiness.mit.edu [accessed 28 October 2013]